Original title:
Left in the Dust

Copyright © 2024 Creative Arts Management OÜ
All rights reserved.

Author: Peter James
ISBN HARDBACK: 978-9908-0-0662-8
ISBN PAPERBACK: 978-9908-0-0663-5

Echoes of Yesterday's Journey

I tripped on my own shoe lace,
A stumble, a laugh, a silly race.
My thoughts were lost in yesterday's haze,
Chasing a bike, on a sunny blaze.

The ice cream man, he sped on by,
I waved hello, he didn't comply.
With sprinkles of joy in my hair so wild,
I pondered life's puzzles, a quirky child.

Traces of a Faded Path

I wandered off down a path so vague,
Only to find my childhood leg leg.
Forgotten treasures, like toys in the grass,
Each step stumbles into a comical class.

The tree I climbed now whispers low,
Dangling nuts, like upside-down snow.
I dance with shadows, twirl and spin,
Where laughter and echoes intermingle within.

When Dreams Stand Still

I snoozed my alarm like a boss of dreams,
Awoke to the sight of my cat's loud screams.
The toast popped up, a charcoal surprise,
No breakfast feast—only smoke in my eyes.

The coffee pot sputters, a gunky old friend,
Reminding me that mornings don't always blend.
Yet here I stand with a grin quite wide,
Laughing at fate, on this bumpy ride.

Beauty in the Remnants

In the cluttered garage, I sought the lost,
A odd-shaped chair, but what a cost!
With laughter, I recall the strange old finds,
A magic carpet ride, in my own mind.

Old records play songs of meaning unclear,
As I shimmy with dust bunnies, full of cheer.
Though remnants might fade, the fun stays alive,
I chuckle at life, oh how we survive!

Amongst the Ruins of Yesterday

Chasing all my dreams that flew,
Fell for candy wrappers too.
Thought I'd find a treasure map,
But found instead a sleeping cat.

Left my socks beneath the chair,
Wandering without a care.
Dust bunnies danced in a line,
My ambitions lost; oh, how divine!

Forgotten jeans with pockets torn,
Where's my jacket? Oh, wait, it's worn.
Yesterday's pizza's still around,
A monument to snacks I found!

Twilight's Lament.

Underneath a lamp's soft glow,
I dropped my sandwich, oh no!
The twilight laughs with purring grace,
As I trip over my shoelace.

Birds sing songs I've never heard,
While I recite the strangest words.
A ghost of dinner haunts my plate,
With leftovers that just won't wait.

Twilight whispers silly schemes,
Like washing dishes with whipped cream.
I raise a toast with empty cups,
To the joy of craziness in ups!

Whispers of Abandonment

Abandoned socks and lonely shoes,
My thoughts wander; I just snooze.
An old toaster makes a scene,
Burnt bread shouts: 'I was pristine!'

Chairs stacked high like towers tall,
I wonder why they gave their all.
A lost remote, where could it be?
Swallowed by the couch, I see!

Dust motes dance in morning light,
I thought I cleaned, but oh, what fright!
Echoes of laughter spill and fall,
A funny case of nothing at all!

Shadows of the Forgotten

In the corner lurks a chair,
Empty pizza box is there.
Shadows giggle in delight,
At my failed attempt to write.

The forgotten teddy on the floor,
Wants a hug—well, who needs more?
Ghosts of snacks in kitchen dark,
Whisper tales of an old spark.

Old homework piles, a curious sight,
Turning into paper kite.
Socks stolen by the laundry beast,
From such fun, I'll never cease!

Solitary Echoes Reverberate

In a room filled with chatter, so loud,
I stand alone, feeling quite proud.
My jokes fall flat like yesterday's bread,
They laugh at my shoes, not words that I said.

Hiding in corners, I sip my drink slow,
While my punchlines wander, taking it slow.
I mime up a storm, no applause in sight,
Guess I'll just share my thoughts with the light.

The Abyss Between Then and Now

Remember those days when we'd dance on our feet?
Now we run marathons just to find something to eat.
Back then we were nimble, so quick and so spry,
Now we groan like old tires when we just try to fly.

With memories sparkling like glitter on skin,
I stumble on echoes of what might have been.
Our past is a comedy, a slapstick affair,
Where my legs seem to vanish, but my socks are still there.

Grains of Time Lost in Space

Tick-tock, the clock's like a playful old cat,
Chasing shadows of moments, where did they scat?
With time like sand slipping, I blink and it's gone,
Now I'm late for my zoom call, where did I don?

The stars blink in laughter, I wave from my chair,
Tangled in puzzles, like I lost a spare pair.
With snacks in my lap and a laugh at my plight,
I chuckle at how I forgot to say goodnight.

The Pathway to Oblivion

Tripped on the way, I fell into glee,
Life's a comedy show and I'm the marquee.
With each little misstep, I gather some dust,
But I prance like a peacock, oh, dance I must!

In a world full of bumps, I find my own groove,
Where laughter's the language and silliness moves.
When plans go awry, I just wink and I smile,
Even chaos can cheer me, even for a while.

Memories in the Corners of the Mind

In a drawer, an old shoe
Forgotten now, it once flew.
Dancing days of youth so bright,
Now it sits to laugh at night.

A sandwich from two weeks ago,
Molded like a work of art, you know.
It stares at me, I can't decide,
To eat it or just run and hide.

Old photos smile, bow ties and booze,
Figures blurry, wearing shoes.
What a time we thought we lived,
Now it's funny, all we give.

Dust collects, memories play,
In a corner, they laugh and sway.
The more I forget, the more they cling,
To remind me of the oddest things.

The Forgotten Symphony of Solitude

In the silence, a phone will ring,
Who could it be? I mean, what a thing!
It's my old friend, clearly I've missed,
But I forgot to add him to the list.

The cat hums softly, takes the lead,
As I sip my tea, I can see a deed.
A concert of one, a fine production,
Lost in the chaos of my own reduction.

The spoon sings back, no one can tell,
If it's happy or under a spell.
In a kitchen dance, I twirl and slide,
Fearing no audience, no one to chide.

So I laugh with dishes, no one to judge,
Messy masterpieces, I dare not budge.
In the forgotten symphony of my day,
I find joy in the sounds of my disarray.

In the Wake of What Remains

Echoes linger in empty rooms,
Where once were laughter and wild plumes.
Now only a chair waits to hear,
The whispers of friends, once so near.

Pineapple pizza, a bold delight,
Once held parties that went all night.
Now just crumbs on the kitchen floor,
They giggle at nights that came before.

Ghosts of socks without their mates,
Have created long-lost debates.
Where did you go? Oh, how could this be?
A mismatched fate for socks and me.

In the wake of what once was grand,
I find humor in all that's planned.
Memories linger like old perfume,
Smiling at chaos in every room.

The Distance of Untrodden Trails

I set out with a map and a frown,
To find the best spot in this quaint town.
But the path led me right to a tree,
Where squirrels held a conference, you see.

With breadcrumbs strewn, I lost my way,
Chasing shadows by end of day.
A wayward cat claimed a sunny seat,
I joined the meeting—oh, what a treat!

The trails untraveled hold their jest,
As every wrong turn became a quest.
In the realm of detours, laughter flows,
Finding the joys in the wild that grows.

So, steer your path with a wink and smile,
For the distance can stretch on a while.
Each twist and turn teaches me new trails,
In this silly life, adventure prevails.

When Time Stands Still

The clock mocks me with its hands,
Ticking slow like molasses bands.
I made my plans to slowly grown,
Yet here I am, just stuck alone.

My coffee's cold, it's now a block,
The milk should've danced like a clock.
But here I sit, a living ghost,
Of all the tasks I love the most.

The cats just laugh, they've got it made,
While I'm a prisoner, time's charade.
The world moves on, a fast parade,
Yet here I dwell, in this charade.

So cheers to moments that refuse,
To move along, to take a cruise.
I'll raise my cup, to stagnant zest,
In the land where time's a jest!

At the Edge of Solitude

I stand alone, but not too keen,
Surrounded by trees, that act like a screen.
They whisper secrets, but do they care?
Got no response, just the chilly air.

My thoughts are loud, they echo fine,
Like a movie scene without the line.
I shout for help, still no reply,
Next time I'll just bring a pie.

In silence, I ponder, what's next to do,
Maybe I'll start a soliloquy too.
But then again, who'd hear my claim?
The squirrels just giggle at my lame game.

So here I am, at solitude's gate,
Attempting to chat with my own fate.
A funny sight, if someone peeked,
We'd all agree, this setup's peaked!

Vestiges of a Vanished Path

Once upon a trail that sparkled bright,
Now just a memory, lost from sight.
I tripped and fell, on what I thought,
Was a garden path, but I was caught.

A picnic planned, but ants have dined,
On all the treats I'd lovingly signed.
With crumbs like confetti, I waved goodbye,
I swear, those bugs had a sly eye.

Nature's comedy, a slapstick show,
As I took a tumble, oh no, oh no!
Laughter erupted from every tree,
A audience pleased, all watching me!

So here I roam, on paths that fade,
Crafting stories that never invade.
Where laughter reigns, I'll let it stay,
And laugh along with the critters all day!

The Weight of Unspoken Goodbyes

You wave your hand, I wave mine back,
But words escape, like a train off track.
A hug is shared, yet no one speaks,
awkward smiles, like hidden peaks.

We stand like statues, frozen in time,
A comical scene, a nursery rhyme.
Your shoe untied, a playful hint,
Still, off we go, to battle the hint.

How do you say, what's on your mind?
When jumbled feelings are hard to find?
So here's a smile, a wink, a cheer,
At least it's clear, we'll meet next year!

So let's embrace this silly plight,
With laughter shared in fading light.
Behind our backs, the bubbles fly,
As we depart, with unsaid goodbyes!

Beneath the Dust, a Story Lies

In the corner, old shoes sit,
With ghosts of dances, each a hit.
The dust bunnies laugh at the scene,
As if they know what might have been.

A book with pages torn and creased,
Whispers tales of a long-lost feast.
Each crumb tells of a hungry lie,
While the dust motes waltz in the sky.

Oh, the memories stuck in a jar,
Of parties where none traveled far.
Laughter echoes, but now it's rare,
As the dust settles everywhere.

So let's dust off that old surprise,
And spin a yarn that never dies.
For hidden treasures are not so far,
Just check the shelf where old shoes are.

The Chasm of What Remains

In the attic, the clutter sways,
Echoing laughter from bright days.
Puzzled faces of dolls so proud,
Waving at us, joyfully loud.

Forgotten games, a dusty clue,
Here's a yo-yo that used to woo.
It tells of tricks and failed attempts,
As we laugh at all the pretense.

Oh, the treasures that time forgot,
Buried beneath a muffin pot.
Each speck of grime hides a tall tale,
Of excitement lost on a lazy trail.

Digging deep into the past,
Find a snow globe, oh what a blast!
It twirls and sparkles while we cheer,
As the dust bunnies draw near.

When Silence Speaks the Loudest

The clock ticks softly, what a tease,
A riddle wrapped in memories, if you please.
Whispers float through the rooms unseen,
Beneath the calm, a raucous scene.

The couch creaks with secrets to tell,
Of sitcoms where awkward moments dwell.
Each dusty corner hums a tune,
As we chuckle at misfortune's boon.

Lurking shadows share a silly jest,
While hidden echoes put us to the test.
In stillness, laughter rings so bright,
The calm before the goofy night.

We tiptoe through what joy might hold,
Past relics of mischief, brave and bold.
In silence, we hear the loudest cheer,
As dust reveals our playful fear.

A Hidden Journey Through Time

Open the door to the past so grand,
A mishmash of memories, all unplanned.
The globe spins tales of places we missed,
While dust clouds form a little tryst.

Faded photos, a funny surprise,
Caught mid-laugh with wide-open eyes.
Each snapshot a puzzle, amusing by chance,
As time ticks forward in a whimsical dance.

Old toys piled high, what a sight,
Daring us to laugh at their plight.
Once adored but now just a rumor,
Obscured by dust, a sweet consumer.

So pack your bags for this comedy ride,
Through time's winding roads where laughter resides.
Lift the veil of the mundane so grim,
And uncover tales both funny and dim.

Withered Leaves of the Heart

My love is like a crumpled hat,
Tossed aside and slightly flat.
Once it sparkled, bright and bold,
Now it lies in the winter cold.

I took you out on a sunny day,
You said my jokes were here to stay.
But summer faded, laughter too,
Now it's just a silly boo-hoo!

We danced on rooftops, oh so high,
Now we just groan and wonder why.
Swept up in a whimsical breeze,
It sure is hard to find our keys!

So here we sit with our shared sighs,
Amusing tales, those goofy tries.
With each joke, we drift on by,
Like lost balloons that touch the sky.

Journey Through the Ashen Ruins

We trekked through ruins, what a sight!
Where dreams once soared to dizzying heights.
Now it's just tumbleweeds and dust,
Yet we laugh, because we must!

I lost my map, you lost your shoe,
But who needs plans when there's fun to pursue?
We drew stick figures on broken walls,
Pretending to host our grandest balls.

The echoes of laughter haunt the halls,
As we ricochet off crumbling walls.
Ghosts of our dreams, they tickle and tease,
Turning our frowns into moments that please.

A field of ashes, but our hearts stay warm,
In silly capers, we weather the storm.
We may be lost, but we find our way,
With giggles and joy, it's our perfect play!

A Canvas of Abandoned Dreams

Once we painted with colors so bright,
Now the canvas is a confusing sight.
Where are the rainbows? Where did they go?
Oh look, a splatter! What a funny show!

We had our plans, oh, grand and wide,
Now we're stumbling, giggling, side by side.
Each brushstroke tells of chaos and cheer,
The mishaps we've lived bring smiles, my dear.

Puddles of paint dance in the street,
An artist's nightmare, these scattered feet.
But laughter erupts in this messy spree,
As we create absurdity with glee.

So here's to dreams, though gone afoot,
Our masterpieces are full of roots.
We may not paint a perfect scene,
Yet it's the laughter that reigns supreme!

The Soft Sigh of a Midnight Road

On a midnight road, we drive with glee,
Singing to tunes that are off-key.
The headlights flicker, shadows play,
What a peculiar, humorous ballet!

We missed the exit, oh what a blunder!
But isn't it funny, this road of wonder?
Through twists and turns, we giggle bright,
In our little car, it feels just right.

Past the blinking signs and empty farms,
We weave our story with all its charms.
Every twist is a tale, a laugh so sweet,
Our journey's delight makes life complete.

With every bump, a chuckle's born,
Through the night sky, our dreams are worn.
Let's steer to laughter, take the scenic route,
On this joyous road, we can't ever lose out!

Flickers of Light in Forgotten Corners

In the attic, a cat takes a leap,
Dusty boxes with secrets to keep.
A long-forgotten toy starts to dance,
As memories swirl in a humorous trance.

The old lamp flickers, it stutters and sighs,
A shadow that winks, what a funny surprise!
Dust bunnies tumble, in a chaotic race,
Chasing the beams like they've found their place.

An old shoe's laces tied in a knot,
It whispers, 'Oh dear, I've forgotten a lot!'
The mirror reflects a smile from the past,
In this quirky nook, memories are cast.

So here's to the laughter from places we roam,
Where time plays tricks in its playful dome.
In corners long dim, where the light shines bright,
We find silly joy in forgotten delight.

Untouched Moments in Time's Grip

A clock ticks loudly, its hands like a tease,
Mocking my plans with a mischievous breeze.
Tea in my cup spills, making a mess,
Time's grip has comically odds to assess.

Old photographs whisper of days full of cheer,
Caught in a frame, they try hard to steer.
When laughter erupts from a sunny facade,
The essence of joy just adds to the odd.

The couch is a portal, where old sit and muse,
Lost in the tales of the socks they refuse.
Beneath the soft cushions lie stories untold,
Waiting to tickle the hearts of the bold.

So shout out to moments that time can't erase,
Even when chaos leaps in a race.
Amidst all the prints, dust still has its role,
In untouched moments, we find humor's soul.

Beyond the Veil of Silence

In a library's hush, a book starts to cough,
'Please don't ignore me, I'm not trying to scoff!'
Pages crack open, like chuckles untold,
As laughter echoes from stories of old.

The wisdom of owls perched high on the shelves,
Exchange tips on giggles and how to be elves.
In this solemn space where silence should reign,
A riot of fun lifts the mundane's chain.

Bookmarks dare say, 'Just flip us and see,'
Comics and riddles join in jubilee.
The ghost of a mime with a wisp of a grin,
Wanders through chapters, inviting chaos in.

So here's to the whispers that tickle our ears,
Beneath quiet creaks, laughter always clears.
In the veil of silence where giggles reside,
We find joy in the places that still try to hide.

The Weight of Yesterday's Dreams

A kite caught in branches, what a sight to behold,
Dreams as light as air but tangled like old gold.
They flutter and flounder, a whimsical quest,
Trying to break free, they need time to rest.

A yo-yo, forgotten, swings back and forth,
Reminds me of laughter that once had great worth.
With each flip and spin, it tells tales so grand,
Of dreams that once danced like grains of fine sand.

In the shadows of alleys, where whispers still bloom,
Old wishes gather dust, filling up every room.
A playful reminder of what laughter can do,
To lighten the heart, give wings to the blue.

So here's to the dreams that stick to our side,
They hang like old socks, with nowhere to hide.
In the weight of the past, humor finds its way,
Transforming regrets into quirky today.

A Journey Stalled

We packed the snacks, hit the road,
But our car chose to corrode.
The engine coughed, a mighty wheeze,
We're marooned under swaying trees.

A raccoon laughed, stole our lunch,
While we sat in a bumpy crunch.
With no Wi-Fi, we tell bad jokes,
Two grown-ups lost, mere silly folks.

The GPS just gave a sigh,
As we waved to a passing fly.
We'll walk miles, but first let's snack,
In this dusty plot, we'll find our track.

So here we are, an epic fail,
With a flat tire and a lonely trail.
But laughter spills as we await,
A tow truck from our twist of fate.

Faded Photographs in the Attic

Old photos hide beneath the dust,
With memories that feel robust.
A fashion choice, quite the display,
From the fads of an ancient day.

Granddad's mustache, larger than life,
Mismatched socks caused family strife.
Mom's disco moves, quite absurd,
In the attic, laughter's heard.

A dog in shades, striking a pose,
Next to Aunt Mabel's floral clothes.
Time stood still in that old box,
With silly faces and quirky mocks.

So we laugh as we dust them off,
Recalling times that made us scoff.
In faded frames, our hearts entwined,
In laughter's grip, old love defined.

Dusty Pages of an Untold Tale

In the corner of the dusty shelf,
A story hides, all by itself.
With coffee stains and pages torn,
Its wisdom rests, a little worn.

A knight who tripped over his sword,
And a dragon who often snored.
Pages whisper, filled with jest,
This saga brings us all the best.

Characters dance in clumsy glee,
A love story lost at sea.
With each turn, the chuckles swell,
Revealing secrets no one can tell.

So let's read on, through dust and more,
In these pages, let laughter soar.
In untold tales of silly grace,
We'll find joy in every place.

Tread Softly Through the Echoes

In an old house, echoes ring,
Where voices linger, softly sing.
Watch your step on the creaky floors,
As laughter hides behind closed doors.

Ghosts of pranks from days gone past,
With mishaps shared, the moments last.
A shadow flicks, a giggle falls,
Through these halls, pure nonsense calls.

Careful now, the cat might pounce,
As we tiptoe, giggle, bounce.
In this maze of silly grace,
We find joy in every trace.

So stroll with me through wit and cheer,
Let echoes ring, let laughter near.
In every step, let vapors blend,
Through ghosts of laughter, joy ascends.

Soul Shadows

In the corner, shadows play,
They dance as if to say,
"You thought we'd tag along,
But we're busy with our song!"

A sock rolls past with flair,
It's lost without a care,
While dust bunnies jump and spin,
Leaving traces of their grin.

The cat looks on, bemused,
By all the things we've used,
A spoon, a hat, a shoe,
Once loved, now faded too.

But laughter fills the air,
For all the stuff laid bare,
In the chaos of our days,
We find joy in stray displays.

Echoes of Abandonment

A chair creaks in the gloom,
Its cushion lost to doom,
Once royal throne it stood,
Now just a piece of wood.

Old pizza in the fridge,
Sitting on the ledge,
Hoping for a dinner guest,
But it's fading with the rest.

Dust on the coffee cup,
But I won't give it up,
It's been my silent friend,
Waiting for the party's end.

Echoes laugh in the night,
"Remember when it was bright?"
Yet here we are, all alone,
In the house we've outgrown.

Whispers of Forgotten Trails

The dog found a long-lost bone,
Barking like he owns the throne,
With each wag, he shows delight,
In treasures out of sight.

Old maps crumpled on the floor,
Tales of where we've been before,
A trail of crumbs, a half-eaten snack,
Leading to nowhere, but we don't look back.

Invisible footprints lean,
On trails that never seen,
Laughter echoes past the gate,
A comedy of our fate.

Come, let's follow the funny signs,
Through grass and over vines,
For every turn we leave behind,
Unleashes joy, what a find!

Where Memories Drift

In the attic, I found a sock,
It whispered tales, oh what a shock,
Once a couple, now a tease,
Searching for its friend with ease.

Boxes stacked in all the nooks,
Filled with stories from our books,
Old toys that squeak a little loud,
Now shyly blending with the crowd.

Coffee stains on the table set,
Reminders of the laughter met,
A napkin penned with dreams untried,
Yet here we are, with arms spread wide.

Where memories flow like a stream,
And life feels just like a dream,
We giggle at the things we lost,
In this adventure, there's no cost.

Dusty Footprints of the Past

In the corner of the hall, there lies a shoe,
It belonged to a walking buddy, quite the view.
With laces tied in knots, a tale of clumsiness,
It dances with dust, in a show of silliness.

Grandma had a knack for tripping on her toes,
Her coffee cup would spill, everybody knows!
We laughed until we cried at her grand display,
Now her footprints linger, leading us astray.

Memories are sticky, like gum on the floor,
Every time we find them, we just want more.
In the attic, laughter echoes like a tune,
Dusty jokes retold beneath the light of the moon.

So here's to the mishaps, the missteps, the grins,
The funny old stories where nostalgia begins.
With every dusty shamble, we take one more leap,
Our wobbly adventures, forever we'll keep.

Silent Roads Untraveled

There's a road not taken, overgrown with weeds,
Where bikes have rusted, forgotten in their creeds.
Left with signs that giggle, saying 'You can play!'
But the path's too silly, we choose not to stray.

The map is quite confused, it shows a froggy leap,
Every step uncertain, as we begin to creep.
With each forward motion, a hop and a skip,
A scenic route somewhere, we never took a trip.

Toss a coin for direction, as vision grows thick,
I swear I spotted Bigfoot, or just a furry trick.
We may not find the treasure that led us down this lane,
Yet laughter fills the air, and it's never in vain.

So let's wander merrily, on these turns unkind,
Create a tapestry of the goofy kind.
The roads unworn may lead us to delight,
In the quirkiest places, let's dance through the night!

Emptiness Among the Ruins

Among the broken bricks, a sofa stands tall,
Covered in thick dust, with a cushiony call.
It's lonely as a cactus with no friends around,
Just waiting for a butt to finally sit down.

An old bicycle lies twisted, begging for a ride,
The tires wish for laughter, but they've long since cried.
Weeds sprout from the spokes, a garden's gentle jest,
A rusted safe nearby holds a monster's treasure chest.

Each corner holds a giggle, as shadows joke with light,
In the ruins of the past, there's always room for spite.
For ghosts of raving parties still peek through the cracks,
Exchanging silly stories while the memory tracks.

So let's reclaim the ghosts, and hang a jester's hat,
For in these quiet places, life is still a chat.
The emptiness is charming, a vibrant kind of fun,
In the ruins of our laughter, the echo's never done.

The Weight of Unsaid Goodbyes

On the tip of my tongue, a farewell gone awry,
We waved with silly hands, but the words just flew high.
Tickling our fancies, we laughed till we dropped,
Yet the goodbyes left hanging, all fluffed and cropped.

A garden full of apricots, we forgot to taste,
Spilled over with wishes, too many to waste.
A hug turned into a dance, an encore in time,
But the silence that followed, didn't rhyme with our chime.

So here we stand smiling, with wishes profound,
In a parade of giggles, where joy is unbound.
A wave and a wink, as we bumble and sway,
With the weight of our laughter lighting the way.

Goodbyes may be tricky, like a riddle or quiz,
But with humor at heart, they're never amiss.
For each chuckle at parting, brings friendship more near,
In the tapestry of moments, let's cheer with a cheer!

Unwritten Stories in the Gravel

Beneath my feet, the pebbles sigh,
Each one holds tales of days gone by.
I trip and laugh, collect my pride,
As stories scatter, like grain of tide.

A runaway flip-flop, a lost sock too,
The gravel giggles at my clumsy woo.
Adventures lost, yet still I roam,
Finding joy in chaos, it's my happy home.

With every stumble, I learn to dance,
The world a stage, I'll take my chance.
Each rock might frown, but I see the jest,
Life's little pratfalls, truly the best!

So here's to the gravel, and all its charms,
A trail of laughter, a path of arms.
Together we tumble, a hilarious mess,
In unwritten stories, I find my success.

Fragments of a Fleeting Moment

A fleeting wink, a bike that squeaks,
Moments slip past, like whispers it speaks.
I chase after clouds, they tease and taunt,
But I find a rainbow, in my silly jaunt.

A nearsighted squirrel, scampers away,
I tried to impress, but he's not here to stay.
Fragmented giggles, scattered like seeds,
Nature's comedy—it truly exceeds!

Snap! There goes time, with a sly little grin,
I'm late to the party, where do I begin?
With snippets of laughter, I gather my gear,
These moments are fleeting, but I hold them dear.

So here's to the laughs, and silly mistakes,
Each moment is precious, whatever it takes.
While time might rush, I'll dance right along,
Fragments of joy, like a whimsical song.

The Deserted Trail's Lament

The trail once busy, now yawns in peace,
Echoes of laughter, have taken release.
Chipmunks now chatter, with nibbles to share,
While I wander on, with dust in my hair.

A lone hiking boot, with laces untied,
Curses abandoned, as nature's my guide.
"Why do we hurry?" the trees seem to say,
As I skip past their whispers, in a silly ballet.

A squirrel steals my snack, with a cheeky bite,
I can't help but chuckle, oh what a sight!
The trail's laments, they tickle my toes,
In this empty stretch, my joy only grows.

So here's to the quiet, the winding away,
The deserted places, where I choose to play.
Nature's own laughter, rings clear through the air,
In the stillness around, I find funny flair.

Unraveled Threads of Memory

Memories dangle, like yarn on a shelf,
Tangled and twisted, I laugh at myself.
Each tug brings a chuckle, a snort or a squeak,
With laughter as my blanket, I wrap up the week.

A fuzzy old sweater, from days long gone,
Mismatched buttons, like a quirky dawn.
I slip and I slide, through stories and crumbs,
As echoes of laughter in my heart drums.

With images fading, yet smiles shine bright,
I gather my yarn, through day and through night.
Each thread a reminder, of giggles and glee,
In unraveled moments, I'm truly free.

So let's stitch together the laughter we find,
In tangled up memories, we get intertwined.
With every bit of yarn, a tale to be spun,
Laughter is timeless, we'll always have fun!

Vanished Smiles in the Breeze

A giggle floats on autumn air,
Like socks that just ran off somewhere.
The wind can't help but wear a grin,
As whispers dance where laughs have been.

Remember when the pie hit Lou?
The bird flew by and laughed, 'How true!'
Now crumbs remain, but oh, that day,
We still can hear those giggles play.

The cat trod soft and stifled purrs,
While slips and trips became a blur.
Each tumble down was such a treat,
We have no shame in our defeat.

So raise a toast to missed high fives,
And moments when we felt so alive.
In the breeze, those smiles take flight,
A sprinkle of joy in the fading light.

Ivy on the Wall of Remembrance

With ivy creeping inch by inch,
It tickles memories, oh what a flinch!
The marbles lost on garden grass,
Where laughter lingered and time would pass.

Once we played hide and seek so well,
Until I stumbled, tripped, and fell.
The hedges knew my every flub,
And giggled back with nature's shrug.

Old pair of sneakers, not so neat,
Each brought home grit, a sticky treat.
The wall remembers, as does the ground,
Each silly slip, each silly sound.

Yet under ivy's thick embrace,
We find the joy in our own space.
So here's to walls that watch and smile,
They've seen us romp and laughed a while.

Remnants of Distant Laughter

A clown dropped pies in the old town square,
With every splat, the chuckles shared.
Yet here we stand, with just a smell,
Of whipped cream and joy that used to dwell.

Tape recorder of the shenanigans,
But all that's left are tiny cans.
And echoes faint of cheerful cheers,
We cling to tales from yesteryears.

The old swing creaks, it knows the names,
Of kids who danced in funny games.
But now it sways all on its own,
And grins with secrets, no more shown.

So let's recall those happy gleams,
And chase our past through silly dreams.
For laughter lingers in distant air,
And we're just left with giggles rare.

A Crooked Pathway of Regret

Down a path that wobbles and bends,
Are stories of fun that never ends.
With laughter caught in crooked signs,
And misplaced shoes in muddy lines.

We ventured forth with gleeful shouts,
Only to find an array of doubts.
A stumble here, a tumble there,
Yet who could frown when life brings flair?

The blossoms giggle as we pass by,
Their whispered jokes make grownups sigh.
And banana peels, oh what a jest,
They trip the brave and give their best.

So wander on this winding track,
With open hearts, there's no turning back.
For every slip, there's joy unfurled,
On crooked paths, oh what a world!

Driftwood Dreams

A piece of wood floats by, all worn,
With tales of shores where it was born.
Seagulls squawk and laugh with glee,
While crabs plan their next big spree.

It dreams of sailing on a breeze,
But mostly lounges with great ease.
A sun-baked hero, not a care,
Both drift and driftwood, quite a pair.

The waves they dance, a wacky show,
As seaweed twirls in a goofy flow.
Together they wade through waves of fun,
Crafting memories 'til day is done.

So here they are, this oddball crew,
With tales of jellyfish and seagull stew.
Floating through life, not a single fuss,
In this salty world, who needs a bus?

The Echoing Silence of Departure

A shoe left behind, what a sight,
Set out on adventures, oh, what a flight!
While socks and slippers snicker with glee,
Chasing after who cares, not even a flea.

The door creaks shut, silence abounds,
With echoes of laughter, silliness sounds.
Cartwheeling chairs in a ghostly dance,
Wondering if the party just missed its chance.

A forgotten hat waves from the shelf,
Wishing for fun, but it's all by itself.
While jackets rustle in a cold breeze,
Yearning for warmth, and perhaps some cheese.

So next time you leap on your roam,
Remember the echoes, the laughter at home.
For all the things left in corners and nooks,
Sure all tell stories that deserve some looks.

When Time Stopped Moving

A grandfather clock, frozen in dread,
Tick-tocks quit, what's up with that head?
It sits there sulking, not making a sound,
While onlookers ponder what's coming around.

Seconds unwind like a tangled string,
As ants take a break, no bustling fling.
The world goes on, but that clock is gray,
Dare we pause too in our busy ballet?

Sunbeams stretch and yawn, oh so slow,
Butterflies giggle, swaying to and fro.
While birds make bets on when it will start,
That lazy clock holds a sleepy heart.

When time finally moves, what will it say?
Will it rush ahead or dance and play?
For now, it rests, a joke in disguise,
In a race against its own sleepy skies.

The Abandoned Garden of Thought

In the garden where wild ideas grew,
Now lies a tangle, overgrown and blue.
Thoughts like weeds, sprouting high,
Chasing butterflies that flutter and fly.

A gnome in the corner, forgotten and grumpy,
Wonders why weeds are now so frumpy.
A scarecrow chuckles, swaying with flair,
Watching dreams take a nap without a care.

Petunias gossip, their colors a riot,
While daffodils duel like they're on a diet.
The paths once clear are now a wild maze,
Where ponderous thoughts lose their bright praise.

Yet in this chaos there's laughter and cheer,
For daydreams wander, drawing near.
In an abandoned patch of messy delight,
Fun blooms freely, day turns to night.

The Road Not Taken

Two paths diverged and I chose wrong,
Now I walk with a duck in a thong.
With crocs on my feet, I trip on my lace,
Hoping to find a more suitable place.

The grass on the left looks greener, it seems,
But it's just a mirage, or so says my dreams.
With each step I take, I stumble and fall,
Chasing my shadow—a comedic brawl.

The signposts are crooked, the compass is weak,
Still, I'm laughing too hard to give it a tweak.
Life's twists and turns, they keep me amused,
Maybe the wrong way's the best to be used.

So here I am, with goosebumps and glee,
A life full of mishaps, oh so carefree!
I'll dance down this path with a jig and a chuckle,
For what's life without joy, and a bit of a shuffle?

Starlight That Fell

Oh look! A star fell right into my pie,
I laughed so hard that I almost did cry.
A sprinkle of stardust on top of my treat,
Is it dessert or a cosmic feat?

I fished for a comet with my trusty old net,
But ended up catching a big, stinky pet.
He danced in the moonlight, all wiggly and bright,
Making wishes for pizza in the pale silver night.

With galaxies swirling in my cereal bowl,
I giggle and munch, letting laughter take hold.
Each bite a new planet, each crunch a new star,
There's joy in this universe, wherever you are.

So here's to the wishes that giggle and snort,
And to the star pies that are never too short.
We'll toast to the cosmos, with crumbs on our faces,
Because life is delicious in all of its spaces!

Shadows of Fleeting Time

The clock's hands are spinning like wild little bees,
While I'm stuck in my chair, still wearing my PJs.
Time tiptoes past, making faces at me,
It giggles and winks, as if mad with glee.

I thought I could catch it, that slippery foe,
But it darted away, just to put on a show.
Now I'm here with my cat, who's snoozing away,
As moments keep dancing, I'm losing the play.

Yesterday waved goodbye, then tripped on a shoe,
It fell into next week, and then lost its crew.
With shadows a-dancing, my fun's just begun,
In the waltz of the hours, I laugh with the sun.

So here's to the shadows that tickle and tease,
In the theater of time, I'm the one with the knees.
Let's skip down this hourglass with whimsy and cheer,
For life is a comedy, so bring on the beer!

The Silence of Recollections

I sat down to ponder, then dozed off for a while,
Right then an old memory came in with a smile.
It whispered sweet nothings, danced on the floor,
But tripped on my shoelace and fell through the door.

"Remember the time we tried to bake bread?"
It said with a chuckle, as flour we shed.
The kitchen exploded in giggles and grime,
And bread? Well, it turned to a coal-black crime!

Oh, the moments we cherished, now funny and bright,
Like wearing pajamas when going out at night.
A parade of those faces, a medley of yore,
Every laugh a new ripple, a joy to explore.

So I'll sit in this silence, let the memories roll,
Each one a soft tickle, delighting my soul.
With mittens on my feet and a smile that won't part,
These silences whisper, and they sing to my heart.

Ghostly Footfalls in the Night

A ghost strayed in with quite the flair,
Tripping on shoes that just weren't there.
The curtains flutter, a chandelier swings,
As laughter echoes, oh what joy it brings!

The broomstick flies with a comical twist,
Chasing after a sock, it just could not miss.
Casper's got moves that would make you grin,
Who knew being spooky could be such a win?

Mysterious whispers in the hallways creep,
But they're just lost shoes that have secrets to keep.
As whispers giggle and shadows play,
Those ghostly footfalls just want to slay!

So if you hear a thud or a squeak,
It's just the ghost trying to sneak a peak.
He's looking for socks, perhaps a warm bed,
But with laughter and mischief, his spirit's well-fed!

A Silent Retreat into Shadows

In shadows thick, the cat takes a leap,
A silent retreat where secrets he'll keep.
Tangled in yarn like a comic ballet,
He dances and twirls, then runs in dismay!

The candles flicker, casting odd shapes,
As he chases his tail, oh what a scrape!
Unspools his plans with a pounce and a sway,
Only to trip on a towel, hooray!

Whiskers twitching with a zoom and a dash,
Through the night, he makes quite the splash.
Silently sneaking, but not really sly,
This cat of shadows just wants to fly!

Yet every retreat brings a new silly chance,
To trip over carpets or play in a dance.
So in the shadows where laughter will bloom,
A retreat into antics dispels all the gloom!

Fading Echoes of a Concluded Story

The book on the shelf has gathered some dust,
Its hero escaped with a twist quite robust.
Pages turn softly, a whisper, a sigh,
As characters wander and wave goodbye.

A dragon left puffing in a cloud of smoke,
While sidekicks plot mischief, it's quite the joke!
With echoes that giggle in every old line,
This story concludes with punchlines divine!

Yet even as twilight settles and glows,
The fun in the pages still bumbles and flows.
With laughter that lingers like shadows at play,
The echoes will dance, keeping boredom at bay!

So grab the old book for a chuckle or two,
And join the adventure where nonsense is new.
With fading echoes that spark joy anew,
A story concluded? It's not really true!

The Memory of an Old Road

An old road winds with tales and delight,
Where bumps and chuckles blend soft with the night.
Once paved with dreams, now a path worn bare,
But laughter lingers in the cool evening air.

Each crack in the pavement tells stories of yore,
Of bikes that fell over and knees that would score.
With trees that gossip and branches that sway,
This road remembers all the games we would play!

Wildflowers bloom where laughter was caught,
As squirrels and critters all weave in the plot.
A memory etched, with a wink and a nod,
This road still whispers, "Isn't life a façade?"

So here's to the pathways that lead us to cheer,
To the silly adventures we hold oh so dear.
In the memory of journeys that echo and glide,
We find joy in the dust where laughter won't hide!

Longing on the Wind

Oh, balloons with no string, they drift away,
Tickling the clouds, wishing they'd stay.
The breeze teases my curls and my hat,
As I chase dreams that will never chat.

A kite tangled high, what a messy sight,
Whispers of past fun now taking flight.
I wave and I shout, yet they just soar,
Leaving me here with my socks, what a chore!

A picnic spread wide, but ants make a feast,
I wave at my sandwich, it's gone, to say the least.
Oh, a bite of my dreams, did you swallow it whole?
I'm left with crumbs of laughter, and a roguish goal!

In the realm of what's "almost," quite close but not near,
With every gust of wind, I chuckle, not fear.
Though they float out of reach, let's have some fun,
Chasing those whims 'til the day is done!

Memories Adrift in Time

A mix of old photos and laughter on rope,
We sat in a circle, all visions and hope.
Then a sneeze from the cat sent our snacks to the air,
Byte-size mishaps, now that's a real scare!

We planned a grand feast, in our wild delight,
Yet flamingo balloons took off with a flight.
Silly hats gone rogue, on friends' heads they dance,
Five seconds of fame in our childhood prance!

Old toys stacked high like a tower of dreams,
Till an elbow nudged and that's when it seems,
They tumbled and fumbled, oh what a sight,
While we rolled on the ground, giggling with might!

Every tick of the clock, a flashback in mind,
Adventures we had are hilariously blind.
And though they are fleeting, these moments we find,
Are memories adrift, but oh so unconfined!

The Silence After Departure

A door that swung shut, what a curious sound,
The echo of laughter that spun all around.
Now I'm sitting alone with a fruitcake so old,
Trying to recall the fun stories told.

The chair still spins; it remembers the glee,
Of wild party nights, and too much iced tea.
Savvy friends have vanished, poof! Like a mist,
Their punchlines and quirks, are terribly missed!

I look at the clock, and it laughs at my plight,
Each tick a reminder of left-out delight.
Confetti on floors, like stars in my space,
Feels like a disco—oh, but there's no trace!

Yet silence is golden, with echoes of cheer,
I dance with old cushions; I hum to the sphere.
With a wink at my fruitcake, still here by my side,
I'll conjure old magic with giggles and pride!

Ghosts of the Unseen

In the hallway, whispers of echoing cheer,
Adventures they had, now silently near.
I tiptoe around, lest I step on their tail,
Can a ghost make cookies? Let's set them to sail!

They play hide and seek, these phantoms of fun,
A laugh here, a giggle, then off they all run.
Through walls, they zoom past in shimmering trails,
Telling tall tales of fantastical fails!

With no shadows seen, still, I hear the delight,
Of pranks and shenanigans lurking each night.
Oh, the spirits of silliness, come out to play,
In a world full of chuckles, they're never away!

So raise up a toast to these friends of the air,
With laughter and joy that we continually share.
For though they are ghostly and sparkle so bright,
They've left us their humor, a dazzling light!

In the Wake of Absence

The donut shop shut its doors with pride,
My morning treat rolled out like a tide.
Chasing crumbs that danced away,
I tripped on memories, had to stay.

My coffee cup holds whispers deep,
Of laughing friends who made me weep.
They left their jokes in every sip,
Yet I'm stuck here on this sinking ship.

The cat in the window mocks my plight,
As I search for laughs in the fading light.
I wave to shadows that steal the day,
While squirrels play tag in their own ballet.

Who knew absence tasted this bittersweet?
Like pie without filling, just a crumby treat.
I'll wear my grin though they're far away,
Creating punchlines for a one-man play.

Unraveled Dreams in the Wind

I lost my shoe, it flew away,
Like my hopes on a windy day.
Chasing it down, I trip and fall,
The dog laughs loud, oh, how I sprawl!

Kites soar high, while I'm left low,
Behind my dreams, like a slow pogo.
Each gust whirls more wishes around,
But my feet feel anchored to the ground.

The ice cream truck plays my favorite tune,
But I'm stuck here chasing a crazed raccoon.
While kids eat sweet, I just scowl,
As my dreams float by like a disheveled owl.

Here's to the thoughts that take to flight,
Twisting like leaves in the fading light.
With laughter blending into the breeze,
I'll find my joy among the trees.

Moments That Slipped Away

I reached for my keys but grasped the air,
Like finding socks that just aren't there.
Moments flip-flop in a manic dance,
While I'm left pondering this wild romance.

The clock ticks loud with a mocking grin,
As I'm busy counting the things I've been.
A sandwich left out, a joke gone stale,
But laughter leaks out like an old mail trail.

I sent my plans on a one-way flight,
They landed somewhere, without a sight.
The memories gathered like dust on a shelf,
And I'm here just laughing at myself.

But silly regrets just tickle my soul,
Like mismatched socks in a bright-eyed shoal.
I'll embrace the folly with every laugh,
Because moments not captured, still make a path.

Reflections in the Fog

The mirrors fog up as I stand and stare,
At all the people who just don't care.
Their polished faces drift like mist,
While I chase reflections I can't resist.

A face in the glass teases with glee,
Or is it just my own, playing tricks on me?
I'm here on a quest for the funny and bright,
But all I find are shadows that bite.

Coffee spills over, my thoughts go awry,
While the world laughs loud, I'm here to comply.
Chasing the echoes of jokes long past,
In this fog of laughter, I'm free—at last!

So here's to the moments that slip and slide,
Like slippery fish that I can't decide.
Through all the confusion, I'll find my cheer,
And dance with the shadows as they disappear.

The Remnant Footprints

In a race but lost my shoe,
My foot met dust, oh what a view!
Left my buddy just to laugh,
He ran ahead, I stuck in half.

With sandy toes and a grin so wide,
I chased him down, my secret pride.
But all that's left is quite a mess,
A footprint trail, I can't confess.

Yet every print shows where I've been,
A comic dance, it seems so keen.
I flip and flop like I'm in fight,
A sight to see, what sheer delight!

So let them jest, let laughter flow,
For dust may stick, but joy will grow.
In tracks we make, we leave it all,
A legacy of slip and fall!

Faded Echoes of Yesterday

Remember when I tried to fly,
With arms out wide, I took off high?
Oh wait, that's just an echoing whack,
I landed face-first, no looking back.

Dust bunnies danced beneath my feet,
As I navigated the clumsy beat.
They laughed as I rolled down the hill,
Yet on my face, there stayed a thrill.

Fading whispers of prideful screams,
Turned to snickers, all in dreams.
Each stumble's a treasure, a twist of fate,
In the hall of mishaps, I now elate.

So let the echoes linger long,
A melody of mishaps, sweet and strong.
For every laugh, a tale unfolds,
In our hearts, the best jest holds!

Ghosts of the Unremembered

Wandering through the dusty lane,
I tripped on nothing, felt no shame.
The air was filled with chuckle and cheer,
Even ghosts of fails found it all dear.

They tease my shoes, worn out and odd,
Each step a haunting, a playful nod.
Together we jest, a phantom parade,
A spectacle of fun like never portrayed.

"Hey, look at that one!" I suddenly shout,
A ghost in a tutu, all in a bout.
Faded memories, but spirits alive,
In laughter and fun, we truly arrive.

So here's to stumbles, to slipping and glides,
In the realm of the unremembered, joy abides.
Every tumble's a ghostly delight,
In the echoes of laughter, we take flight!

Stranded on the Sandy Shore

I thought I'd tan, all in repose,
But quickly learned, I've got big toes!
They poked the sand, a wiggly dance,
I laughed so hard, forgot my stance.

With each wave crashing, I lost my hat,
A seagull snatched it, imagine that!
Now I'm just here with a big ol' grin,
Dust and feathers, the perfect win!

The shore is littered with treasures galore,
Old flip-flops and shells on the floor.
"Behold!" I cried with a glorious shout,
"This sandcastle's mine," with a puff, no doubt!

And though I'm lost in this playful mess,
I'm stranded here, I must confess.
For laughs and giggles, I've found my core,
Life's a beach, oh, I adore!

Forgotten Dreams Beneath the Stars

There once was a dream made of cheese,
It rolled away with the morning breeze.
I chased it through fields of yellow and blue,
But found only crumbs, oh what shall I do?

My pillow's a stage for a snoring star,
It hums a sweet tune from afar.
Each night it invites my lost hopes to sway,
Yet all they do is dance and decay.

The moon winks at me, giggling loud,
As I trip over wishes, feeling quite proud.
I grasp at the beams, all shiny and bright,
But they slip through my fingers, just out of sight.

So here I sit, counting sheep in an ode,
To dreams that went north while I stayed on the road.
With laughter in hand and a heart made of fluff,
I scatter my dreams, hoping that's enough.

Scattered Seeds of Loss

A garden once bloomed with thoughts from my mind,
But weeds took over, oh how unrefined!
I planted some hope, then lost track of time,
Now I'm stuck pulling roots, and making this rhyme.

The plans I had sown like seeds in the ground,
Have sprouted into a circus, oh what a sound!
The rabbits are juggling, the squirrels are grinning,
While I stand confused, wondering where I'm spinning.

Each petal that fell told a joke to the breeze,
And my thoughts floated up, with the greatest of ease.
Now laughter erupts from the patches of green,
As I search for a carrot, but only find beans.

So here's to the chaos, a toast with some juice,
To all the wild dreams that loosened their noose.
Though scattered and lost, they still make me chuckle,
In my whimsical field, I find joy in the rubble.

The Remains of What Once Was

A sandwich pretended to be a delight,
But mold took the stage, a terrible sight.
I tossed it away, with a theatrical flair,
Just like my diet, vanished into thin air.

The remnants of yesterday's laughter still cling,
To the walls of my fridge, where lost treasures sing.
With leftovers talking about their past fame,
While I sit in my chair, thinking of blame.

The cookies I saved now barter for cheese,
Demanding a party, oh please, oh please!
I'll throw in some chips and a soda or two,
While the remains of that pasta plot mischief anew.

So here's to the moments that slipped through my grasp,
To the humor I find in a forgotten clasp.
As I dig in the fridge, brimming with pride,
I celebrate chaos, and laugh at the tide.

Solitude's Accompaniment

In a room full of echoes, I twirl like a sprite,
With socks on my hands, oh, what a sight!
I dance with my shadow, and it steals the show,
We spin and we laugh, while the world doesn't know.

My thoughts play the drums in a solo parade,
As solitude giggles, unbothered, unfrayed.
I sip from a teacup that's dressed like a hat,
And wonder if anyone notices that!

The walls start to chatter, they whisper my name,
In a chorus of sarcasm, it's all just a game.
I trip over laughter and roll on the floor,
While solitude winks, asking me for more.

So keep me in my bubble, where weirdness reigns,
With whimsical tales and no tiny chains.
For in this bright silence, I'll dance till I rust,
With my fanciful dreams, embracing the dust.

Unseen Trails and Untold Stories

In the woods where no one roams,
The trees tell tales of ancient gnomes.
They giggle and laugh as they hide away,
While squirrels plot mischief for the day.

With each twist and turn, secrets abound,
A treasure map lost, not a peep found.
Chasing shadows that dance with delight,
We question our wisdom, is it day or night?

Footprints lead nowhere, just dust in the air,
We stumble and mumble, oh, what a snare!
The compass spins wildly, it must be a joke,
As we chase after laughter amidst all the smoke.

So here's to the trails that we wander offbeat,
In the belly of nature, full of life's treat.
With each chuckle and snicker from unseen friends,
Our adventure is sweeter, the humor never ends.

As the Dust Settles

When the dust finally settles, what do we see?
A pile of old socks and a recipe.
Forgotten spaghetti out dancing with bugs,
Got more twists and turns than my old pair of slugs!

We leap from the chaos, knee-deep in cheer,
Finding lost toys as we guffaw with fear.
Who knew the vacuum could hide such a mess?
A mythical land beneath layers, no less!

So we laugh at the remnants of what once was grand,
A kingdom of clutter we don't understand.
Yet each little item tells stories of past,
From a broken old watch that no longer lasts.

Now, with giggles and grins, we clean up this place,
Finding old treasures, we just can't embrace.
As the dust settles down, we nod in accord,
This house is a circus, with fun as its lord!

The Path of Forgotten Songs

There's a road paved with tunes that no one hears,
With melodies trapped in the dust of old gears.
Each note waves hello while hiding behind,
As we trip on the lyrics, so whimsically blind.

A chorus of crickets sings out of tune,
While the moon rolls its eyes at the raucous festoon.
We hum along awkward, trying to rhyme,
To the beat of the earth, so silly, no crime!

So grab your kazoo and your wild tambourine,
Let's march like a band of invisible sheen.
With laughter in step, and mistakes all around,
We're the jesters of music lost in the sound.

As we dance on the path where the forgotten belong,
We embrace each misnote in this silly sing-song.
With hearts a'flutter and joy in our throng,
We found entertainment where laughter is strong!

Whispers from a Vanishing Past

In shadows that linger, whispers unfold,
Of antics from yesteryear, stories retold.
A grandfather clock with a pocket of dust,
Tickles our senses with echoes of trust.

The attic's alive with cobwebs that sway,
As moths take their flight to reminisce play.
Old shoes trod lightly, forgetting their path,
While memories dance, stirring up a good laugh.

We sift through the laughter, and giggles we find,
In corners where memories tenderly unwind.
Every faded photograph brings back a cheer,
Of moments immortal, though time disappears.

So here's to the laughs filtered through time,
As we cherish the quirk in this playful rhyme.
With whispers of joy that refuse to pass,
Our hearts remain full, though the moments may last.

Strands of Memory in the Wind

Balloons of laughter float away,
Chasing squirrels and dreams at play.
Old candy wrappers swirl and spin,
Reminders of where we've been.

Cracked sidewalks tell the tales anew,
Of lives once shared, now few but true.
The wind plays tricks with our hairstyle,
What once was serious, now is a smile.

Tickled by a passing breeze,
Chasing thoughts like silly leaves.
We trip on memories—oh what fun!
Each step is silly, and we run!

Time does its dance, hilarious and wild,
With every chuckle, we're beguiled.
So here we are, just you and me,
In windy joy, forever free!

Fluttering in Sunlight

Butterflies flap in a dizzy twirl,
While dandelions throw their pearls.
We bounce along this path of glee,
Frolicking like kids, wild and free!

Sunshine giggles on our faces,
As we race at bouncing paces.
A squirrel scowls and flicks his tail,
As we tell him our best tale.

Cups of lemonade spill with cheer,
We splash the warmth, no hint of fear.
In this silly, sunlit dance,
Who cares if we might miss our chance?

Look, a shadow—oh wait, just me!
This game of tag, so carefree!
Every flutter and dance so bright,
We laugh until the stars ignite!

Unseen

Invisible threads that tie us tight,
We laugh and jiggle, oh what a sight.
With winks and nods that no one can see,
Like invisible gnomes having tea!

A wink to the past, a nudge to the now,
As we dance like cats on a prowl.
The world may ignore our quirky ways,
But in our bubble, it's a merry play!

We mime our stories, oh what a show!
Around us, the confused crowd aglow.
With laughter echoing from afar,
We're the stars, despite who we are!

So here's to the unseen, the quirks and the cheers,
Keeping us giggling throughout the years.
Let's raise a toast—imagine, oh what fun,
In this invisible dance, forever spun!

Trail of Forgotten Whispers

Beneath the moon, our secrets bloom,
The whispers echo in the gloom.
We stumble on tales, slightly askew,
Laughing at things we once thought true.

Each corner turned, a stuttered phrase,
A jumbled map of forgotten ways.
We trip and giggle on memories past,
While shadows dance, they're fading fast!

The chatter of crickets plays a tune,
While fireflies giggle under the moon.
A shuffling breeze sweeps up our raucous thoughts,
In our funny march, it's chaos we've sought!

So let's skip along this echoing gun,
Through laughter and whispers, we've just begun.
To roam the path of dust and delight,
In the trail of the funny, we'll dance through the night!

Dusk's Embrace on Lonely Hearts

When the sun dips low, we frolic and play,
As shadows stretch in a humorous sway.
Each sunset chuckle, a warm embrace,
A brilliant swipe of colors we chase.

Lonely hearts in a silly dance,
Unruly dreams give love a chance.
With sighs of joy and hiccuped laughs,
We create our own twisted crafts.

Dusk giggles in hues of gray,
As we trip through twilight, come what may.
In the waltz of stars, we find our way,
Together we'll hum the night away!

So here's to the hearts that twirl and spin,
In the funny dusk where all begins.
With laughter echoing, we'll sweetly part,
In the embrace of dusk, it warms the heart!